G000141729

ECONOMICS

IN

24 HRS

Great Pillars Publications

TABLE OF CONTENTS

INTRODUCTION

In the summer of 2013, perhaps, owing to the grim economic situations all over the world marked by huge economic disparities among different groups of people, a non-uniform prosperity everywhere, and the existence of a myriad of populace in the state of economic stagnation in almost every country, we were motivated to take a deep interest in knowing about why these things happen, and how the underlying economics of the world including these phenomena work.

And to understand the underlying economics from the very basics, we carefully chose many economics books and other useful information which were available on the internet and elsewhere. We read a number of books, articles, essays, and other materials which were written on economics and its history over the last few centuries.

With the help of these books and resources, we tried to understand how early men interacted with nature and among themselves, and how the mankind, as a society in some places, began producing useful things and progressed to become very prosperous in some parts of history. And in other times and places, how some societies devolved into a state which bred ignorance and inequality of all kinds and ultimately collapsed.

We found some good knowledge in different areas of economics, but we did not find any convincing knowledge about the real nature of money, its value and purchasing power, and how banking and inflation affect it. We tried diligently to find out the real concepts of money, its effects on economy, and how its manipulation over the course of history has led to the present day system of banking and inflation.

After reading the books and other information, though we found some principles of economics to be logical, many were vague and not founded on reasoning. And it was quite difficult for us to develop a clear comprehension about the overall nature of economics, and its concepts remained nebulous to us as most of the existing findings of economics were not based on objective logic.

And so we delved deeper into the works of well-known and not so well-known persons who had contributed to the field of economics. After we had acquired adequate knowledge of economics from these works during the period of four years between May, 2013 and November, 2017, in 2018, we developed our own concepts of economics especially on money and its purchasing power, and on the basis of our concepts, we were able to describe many economic phenomena, for example how the addition of new money will affect the purchasing power of the people in an economy.

We thought that a simple book which covers the basics of economics on a logical foundation and objective reasoning was much needed which would not only be easy for a layperson to comprehend, but also be useful for those people who think that the presently available knowledge of economics is sufficiently accurate.

In this book, we have tried to include many of those concepts which we found to be based on objective logic and sound reasoning. We have included a theory on the concept of money and its relative purchasing power which we have developed on the basis of our observation of the present world and its history over the last few centuries. Some existing concepts which we have improved are also presented in this book.

After reading this book, a person will be able to understand how the economy of the world works from the production and exchange of goods and services to the effects of money and banking. The readers of this book will get the concepts, both theoretical and practical, about the real value of money and its purchasing power. They will also be able to develop their own economic perspective about the value of a good or service, factors of production, markets, purchasing power, banking, inflation and its effects, etc.

Since the nature of this book is to give its readers the very foundational knowledge of the workings of economics, the readers of this book will find it quite useful in making good economic decisions for themselves and even in developing their own views about many economic phenomena including the real reasons of present economic situations in different parts of the world and how they can be improved.

We have tried to keep the length of this book short and the language very easy to comprehend, and we have also tried to provide definitions of the terms which are often encountered in the study of economics. Though we have tried to eliminate all errors from this book, some errors might still have remained in the book. We will be grateful to those who find any of the remaining errors and share them with us and we will try to remove those errors in the later editions of this book.

1.

MEANING OF ECONOMICS: THE INTERACTIONS

The interaction between a man and his environment, the interactions among members of humankind, and all the activities related to these interactions constitute the empirical and practical aspects of economics. And the study of these interactions as a science is called economics.

A man might interact with his environment in great many ways, for example he can pick an apple from its tree, he can catch a fish from a river, or he can extract gold from the earth.

A man playing poker with his friend, two sumos wrestling, a mother giving gifts to her child, two men exchanging clay potteries and duffel coats, or a man purchasing a white horse from a horse seller are some interactions between men.

2.

THE BEGINNINGS

THE ENDEAVOUR FOR SUBSISTENCE

When mankind first found himself on Earth, what did he do? Survival was his immediate concern. To survive, he tried to consume what was available in his immediate environment. With experience, he found that the things such as air, water, fruits, fish, animals, plants, etc. were necessary for his healthy survival.

The changes in weather, strong winds, lightning, rains, snowfall, the difference between day and night temperatures, and humidity caused Man to find something to cover and protect himself and some safe place which he could use as shelter.

To cover and protect himself from

uncomfortable weather, he used leaves and barks of trees, and skins or hides of animals. To shelter himself, he searched for caves, or hollows in big tree trunks. Some men worked to make huts using branches of trees, clay, and stones.

When the early men fell ill, got wounds, or suffered insect bites, they tried different parts of plants, herbs, trees, etc. to find out if these things could be used to treat their diseases.

With time they got experienced and acquired knowledge about the benefits and medicinal values of different parts of plants, animals, other natural substances, and their derivatives.

Man also identified natural energy sources

such as the sun, wind, moving water, and fuels, for example wood, coal, etc. These energy sources were utilized for diverse purposes.

They used sunlight for heating and lighting their homes. Wood fire was used for the purposes of cooking, heating, and lighting. The energy of moving water and wind were used in transportation over water.

The early men observed some essential factors of subsistence, namely air, water, food, cloths, shelter, medicines, energy, and a conducive environment for healthy living.

THE MASTERY OVER SUBSISTENCE

Since the early men were able to observe what activities were most important for their healthy survival, they started learning those activities, for example digging wells, purifying water, fishing, rearing and hunting of animals, growing food and medicinal plants, making clothes, building houses, igniting fire, using energy, and so on.

With time and experience, they were able to produce not only for themselves and their families, but they could now offer the surplus produce to their friends and their neighbours as gifts, or exchange their produce with the produce of others.

3.

PRODUCTION: THE BEGINNING OF ECONOMIC ACTIVITIES

Anything, before it can be consumed, or gifted, or exchanged for some other thing, must either be available in nature in a directly usable form or must have been produced by Man prior to its existence. There cannot be any consumption before production, and so we can say that production is the beginning of all economic activities.

Production is any activity which transforms things, tangible or intangible, into things of desired value or utility. Production is a man-made process of transformation, and it does not bring into existence something from nothing; that is to say, it does not create something out of nothing.

THE PRODUCTS: GOODS AND SERVICES

GOODS

A good is any tangible thing which can provide some utility or value to a person. Goods may be natural or man-made, for example oranges, milk, eggs, tomatoes, spinach, radish, carrot, chicken, fish, mustard seeds, olive, cotton, steel, cement, bricks, cars, laptops, airplanes, and many more.

Some goods, for instance e-books, spreadsheets, videos, music, and software, though intangible in nature are stored and used on a physical electronic device. These goods are called e-goods or digital goods.

SERVICES

A service is any action or activity performed by one or more persons which provides some utility or satisfaction to some other person or persons. For example, a doctor may provide his services to a person by examining his body and prescribing medicines.

Services are intangible and must be provided by one or more persons with or without the help of an instrument or a device. A jewellery designer may offer services to his clients by designing a piece of jewellery with the help of hammers, pliers, magnifiers, etc.

Services are produced and consumed at the same time. Unlike goods which can be produced, stored, and consumed at different times, services are consumed at the time of production.

For example, while a hairstylist is providing his services of cutting, coloring, and styling the hair of his customer, the services are being consumed by the customer at the same time.

COMMODITY

Any good whose individual units are mutually interchangeable irrespective of who produced it is called a commodity. Gold bar of a specific dimension and weight is an example of commodity.

CONSUMPTION

Consumption is the activity or action of using a good or service. Eating chocolates, talking on a mobile phone, using a car for travelling, playing with a basketball, playing video games on a console, watching movies in a theatre are some examples of consumption.

FACTORS OF PRODUCTION

To have a good understanding of how something is produced, we should have the knowledge of things which are absolutely necessary for production and without which it would be impossible to produce anything.

The essential requirements of production are called factors of production.

So far, we have been able to observe five factors of production, namely natural resources, labor, capital goods, time, and conducive conditions which are required in different processes involved in production.

NATURAL RESOURCES

Natural Resources consist of physical space and other material resources which exist in nature without any action of mankind. They include all the naturally occurring things such as air, water, sunlight, land, vegetation, animals, energy sources, and various other substances.

All production processes require a

combination of physical space and other natural resources.

Physical space is the naturally occurring space or region in which production can be carried out, and it includes the earth's surface, the region below the earth's surface, and the region above the earth's surface.

Consider the production of lettuce. A farm land for the agriculture of lettuce provides the physical space. In this case, other natural resources required are air, water, sunlight, and soil which provides nutrients and support.

In the production of steel, land provides the physical space where the steel plant is set up. Iron ore, carbon, and some other elements are the natural resources used to make steel.

LABOR

Labor includes all physical and mental efforts of mankind for the purpose of producing goods and services. Examples include the works and services of all kinds of workers and professionals including entrepreneurs.

CAPITAL GOODS

All goods which are used or which aid in the production of other goods and services are called capital goods for those activities of production. Fishing nets used for fishing, printing machines used for printing books and newspapers, generators for producing electricity, laptops and mobile phones for developing software are some examples of capital goods.

Some capital goods may be of an intangible nature. These include all kinds of knowledge which help in production. The knowledge of science, economics, and technology are some examples.

Capital goods are sometimes also called producer goods because they are used by producers to produce other goods or services.

A good can be a producer good for one person and a consumer good for some other person. For example, a cheese pizza offered by a restaurant is a producer good for the restaurant owners, but it is a consumer good for the person buying it.

In any production process, some capital

goods may get used up quickly and some may take years to get used up completely. For example, in an airline service, the aviation fuel used in an airplane gets used up frequently whereas the airplane itself can be used for years before it is taken out of operation.

Capital goods can be used to increase the productivity of production.

TIME

Any process, whether natural or man-made, takes time. Production is a man-made process of transformation and so it also takes time. We can say time is a factor of production.

The time taken in natural processes such as

formation of fruits cannot be altered easily, but in man-made processes of production, the time to produce may be decided by the producer.

Time is usually allocated for different stages of production and almost every producer tries to allocate an optimum amount of time for producing a good or service.

CONDUCIVE CONDITIONS

Tea is usually cultivated in regions having a warm and humid climate. It also requires a specific amount of rainfall. This shows that the production of tea requires certain conducive conditions to be carried out.

The conditions may be natural or man-made. For example, to melt steel, a very high temperature is required. Here, the high temperature required is a conducive condition to melt steel.

Without the conducive conditions, the processes of production cannot take place. So, the set of conditions, taken collectively, which is conducive to the different processes of production is also a factor of production.

The different factors of production are independent from each other and are required in various combinations to produce a good or service.

After production, a good or service is usually consumed by the person who produced it, or it is gifted to family, friends, or some other person, or it is exchanged for another good or service produced by some other person or persons.

4.

THE VALUE OF A GOOD OR SERVICE

The value of a good or service, as perceived by a person, is not an intrinsic property of the good or service. It also does not depend on the cost of production or the amount of effort made to produce the good or service.

Value of a good or service is subjective. Different persons may value the same good or service differently. The value, utility, usefulness, or satisfaction gained from the same good or service may be entirely different for different persons.

For example, if people have to choose what they like most from the three varieties of cheese, namely mozzarella, parmesan, and ricotta, some may like one variety the most while others may choose a different variety.

We may find that some people like

mozzarella the most whereas some other people like parmesan more than mozzarella. We can say, people value a piece of mozzarella cheese subjectively.

In general, we see that people value the same good or service subjectively.

VALUE DEPENDS ON CONTEXT

The same person, under different circumstances, may not value the same goods and services equally. For example, if a coffee lover from a place where the weather is normally cold goes to a place having hot weather, he may choose some cold drink like a green tea smoothie over a cup of hot coffee.

We can say that even for the same person,

the value of the same good or service may change depending on the context.

VALUE OR UTILITY DEPENDS ON END

A person uses a good to satisfy his ends, for instance he can use his car to travel from one place to another. Here, the good used is car and travelling is the end which can be satisfied by the car.

If a stock of good is available to a person in such a way that every individual unit of the good in the stock is identical to every other unit and can provide the same service to the person, then the number of identical goods in the stock is called the supply of the good for the person.

For example, if a person has ten identical cherry ice cream cups, then the supply of the ice cream cups to the person is ten units. If the stock contains only one good then the supply of the good is one unit.

Now, let us consider that a person buys 1 litre or 1000 ml of milk for a day's consumption. The supply of milk is 1000 ml. He plans to allocate 500 ml for curd, 250 ml for coffee, and the remaining 250 ml for milkshake.

The most important end which he wants to satisfy is making curd using the milk. His second and third most important ends are making coffee and making milkshake respectively.

1. 500 ml for curd

2. 250 ml for coffee

3. 250 ml for milkshake

The portion of milk which he allocates for satisfying his most important end, which is making curd, provides the highest usefulness or utility to him. In the same way, the next 250 ml for coffee provides him the second highest utility. And the next 250 ml for milkshake provides him the third highest utility.

One day, one of his friends comes to visit him, and he makes coffee using 250 ml of the milk and drinks it. Now the person is left with only 750 ml of the milk and therefore he cannot fulfill all his three ends. He decides to use the remaining milk for satisfying his first and second ends which are making curd and making coffee respectively, and he gives up his third end which is milkshake.

From the above example, we can see that a person uses the stock of a good to satisfy his ends. A person usually ranks his ends in the order of their importance to him and allocates different parts of the stock to satisfy his different ends.

If the stock of a good is limited to a person in such a way that he can fulfil only some of his ends using the supply of the good, then he will fulfil his most important ends using the supply, and his other less important ends will remain unfulfilled.

5.

EXCHANGE

DIRECT EXCHANGE

Two persons who own two different goods may exchange their goods if both of them value the other person's good more than they value their own good. When two persons exchange their goods or services directly, this may be called direct exchange or barter.

For example, a person A is having a porcelain tea set and a person B is having a silk coat. If A values the silk coat more than his porcelain tea set, and B thinks that the tea set would be more valuable to him than his coat, then A and B may exchange or barter their goods.

MARKET

A market is a place where two people exchange their goods or services.

INDIRECT EXCHANGE

Let us consider a case in which three persons A, B, and C are the owners of oranges, apples, and guavas respectively.

A wants guavas, B wants oranges, and C wants apples. We can observe that A and B cannot exchange their fruits directly as A wants guavas but B can only offer apples. In the same way neither B and C nor A and C can exchange their fruits directly.

PERSON	OWNS	WANTS
A	ORANGES	GUAVAS
B	APPLES	ORANGES
C	GUAVAS	APPLES

We can easily conclude that direct exchange cannot take place in this case. However, indirect exchange is possible if A exchanges his oranges with B's apples and then exchanges the apples with C's guavas.

EXCHANGES OVER TIME

Consider a case where there are two persons, one of them is a producer of wheat and the other is an owner of sugar. The producer of wheat needs sugar, but he cannot offer wheat at present since his wheat can only be harvested after a month.

The wheat producer makes an offer to the sugar owner that he will give him 40 pounds of wheat after one month if he gives him 20 pounds of sugar now. The sugar owner accepts the offer and asks for a contract note or certificate mentioning that the wheat producer will give him 40 pounds of wheat on demand after one month.

From the above example, we can see that exchanges of goods and services can be made over time.

6.

MONEY: COMMON MEDIA OF EXCHANGE

When a group of people decide that while offering their goods and services they will accept some agreed upon things in exchange, the agreed upon things become common media of exchange and are called money in their group.

At different times in different parts of the world diverse things were used as common media of exchange or money. Some prominent things such as sugar, tea, cowrie shells, copper, silver, and gold were used as money.

TYPES OF MONEY

COMMODITY MONEY

When actual pieces of a commodity are used as a common medium of exchange, the pieces of commodity become commodity money. For example, gold and silver pieces measured by their weight, specific varieties of cowrie shells measured by their count, etc.

Any piece of a commodity is valued in varied ways by people mainly because of its material content, properties, and uses. We can call this value as the material value of the commodity.

When a commodity is used as money, it

acquires some additional value owing to its use as a common medium of exchange. This value may be termed as money value or exchange value of the commodity when it is used as money.

REPRESENTATIVE MONEY

Representative money is a certificate which represents some quantity of an actually existing commodity and is accepted in exchanges as equivalent to the commodity money itself.

For example, gold or silver certificates used as money represent some definite amounts of gold or silver. It means, in addition to their use as money, they also act as a claim on some definite amounts of gold or silver.

FIAT MONEY

Fiat money is a type of money which derives its value from an arithmetic or numerical denomination which is usually assigned or marked on a piece of paper or some other thing, and it is not backed by any commodity.

Fiat money derives its exchange value from its assigned value and not from the material of which it is made. On identical pieces of paper, different denominations can be assigned.

For example, in the system of modern fiat currencies, government and its agencies assign some denomination usually on a piece of paper, plastic, or metal discs called coins.

ESSENTIAL PROERTIES OF MONEY

The commodity which is accepted as a common medium of exchange must be easily divisible into smaller units. For example, gold, silver, and copper are easily divisible commodities.

Money must also have the fungibility property. A commodity is fungible if its individual units are interchangeable. For example, two pieces of ten grams of pure silver can be interchangeably used for exchanging with a good or service.

The material of which money is made must be durable. It means it can be used for a long duration of time without getting damaged by corrosion, wear, pressure, etc.

MEASURE OF MONEY

Commodity monies are usually measured by some of their natural properties such as mass or weight and count. For example, gold and silver are measured by their weight whereas cowrie shells are measured by counting the numbers of a specific variety.

Unlike commodity monies, fiat money is measured by the value assigned by some decree of government. The value assigned in this case is not a natural property of the material used in the fiat money.

MONEY PRICES

The amount of money paid by a person to the seller for a good or service is the money price of that good or service for that exchange. Money prices may be different for different purchases by different people involving the same good or service.

A producer or an entrepreneur, when he first launches his product in a market place, sets a price as per his calculations which may involve the cost of production, prices of similar products in the market, and how much buyers may be willing to pay. This price can be called the offered price.

People purchase a good or service at the offered price if they value the good or service more than the offered price that they have to pay. Different buyers may value the same good or service differently even if they are offered at the same price. Prices are not an objective measure of the values of different goods and services.

The entrepreneur may have his expectations about the quantity of goods or services which he will be able to sell at the offered price in a duration of time. Depending on how people react to the product at the offered price, the producer may accordingly adjust the offered price or the quantity to be produced.

MONEY-SUBSTITUTES

Things which are accepted as money and can replace money in all transactions involving money are called money-substitutes. Money-substitutes are equivalent to money and are usually issued by banks.

For example, in old times, the certificates of gold and silver issued by banks to the depositors of gold and silver became money-substitutes and were used as money along with gold and silver.

In modern days in almost all countries, if paper currency is considered as money, then balances in deposit and loan accounts may be regarded as money-substitutes and are used as money.

7.

THE VALUE OF MONEY

A seller of a good or service takes money in exchange for his good or service only when he believes that he will be able to buy other person's good or service with the money he receives.

The part of total money in an economy owned by a person is his claim on a part of the total wealth which is available for purchase in the economy at a time.

For a deeper understanding, let us imagine an economy in which the total money is M at a time which is equal to the sum of the monies owned by every person, and the total purchasable wealth at that time is W.

For simplicity, let us assume that the total purchasable wealth W exists in such a way that it is distributed uniformly over its volume.

Now, suppose a person has m money which is a part of total money M in the economy.

If at any instance of time, every person having some money wants to get a share of the total purchasable wealth W, then the wealth W will be distributed to all persons in the proportion of the money owned by them.

Total money M will be exchanged with total wealth W which means M will purchase W.

1 unit of money will purchase $1/M$ part of the wealth W.

m units of money will purchase m/M part of the wealth W.

We can observe that any person having m

money will get m/M part of the total purchasable wealth W for his money. We may call the ratio m/M, the relative purchasing power of the money m.

Now, let us consider a simple example. On an island there are 11 persons, and the total money in their island economy is 100 units.

For simplicity, suppose 5 persons have 8 units money each, 3 persons have 10 units money each, and 2 persons have 15 units money each. The remaining 11th person does not have any money but has 100 ounces of gold which he wants to sell for money.

At some instance of time, the total purchasable wealth consists of only the 100 ounces of gold which the 11th person wants to sell for money, and the ten persons having money want to buy a part of the gold with their money at the same time.

The total 100 units of money will buy the 100 ounces of gold. It means 1 unit of money will buy 1 ounce of gold. Therefore, each of the 5 persons having 8 units money will get 8 ounces of gold. Similarly, each of the 3 persons having 10 units money will get 10 ounces of gold, and each of the 2 persons having 15 units money will get 15 ounces of gold.

This shows that a person gets the part or share of the total purchasable wealth which is proportional to the ratio of the money owned by the person to the total money in the economy.

In the above example, each of the 5 persons got 8/100 part of the gold, each of the 3 persons got 10/100 part of the gold, and each of the 2 persons got 15/100 part of the gold.

RELATIVE PURCHASING POWER OF MONEY

To comprehend the real value of money, the understanding of relative purchasing power is essential.

The relative purchasing power of the money owned by a person is the ratio of his money to the total money in the economy at a time. It can be calculated as the ratio m/M where m is money owned by a person and

M is the total money in the economy.

This ratio *m/M* represents the part of the total purchasable wealth which the owner of *m* money will get when every person wants to purchase a part of that wealth with their money at a time in the economy.

If in an economy, the total money is 200 units and a person has 10 units money, then his relative purchasing power will be 10/200 which is equal to 0.05.

Now suppose the money owned by him increases to 100 units, but at the same time the total money in the economy has also increased to 2000 units. His relative purchasing power in this case will be 100/2000 which is again equal to 0.05.

The ratio of 0.05 in both cases shows that

there is no change in the relative purchasing power of the person even when his money has increased 10 times because the total money in the economy has also increased 10 times simultaneously.

The money m owned by a person represents only the nominal value, but the real value can be measured by calculating the relative purchasing power m/M.

We can conclude from the definition of relative purchasing power that the sum of the relative purchasing powers of all the people in an economy at a time is always equal to one.

The sum of relative purchasing powers of the people can be written as below.

$$m_1/M + m_2/M + m_3/M + \ldots + m_n/M =$$

$1/M(m_1 + m_2 + m_3 + \ldots\ldots + m_n)$

$= M/M = 1$

8.

BANKING

HISTORY OF BANKING

There exist many speculations about the origins and the history of banking which include the speculations on how the deposit and loan functions of banking evolved with time.

For example, in old days, when agriculture and production of food grains were prevalent, some people, usually farmers, who had surplus food grains used to lend grains to merchants and traders who travelled long distances to sell their goods and services.

During the same time, some warehouse owners used to accept deposits of the surplus produce of farmers for some charge. It is speculated that some warehouse owners sometimes loaned the grains deposited with them to other people for some interest.

The warehouse deposit and the lending of grains emerged independently. The examples above show how the deposit and loan functions of banks might have originated in old times.

GOLD-MONEY AND BANKING

While gold was evolving as a common medium of exchange, its use as money was becoming popular and people started using it for most of the exchanges in markets.

As people started to keep more and more amounts of gold in their houses and with themselves while travelling, they might have felt that it was quite inconvenient to carry gold in large quantities owing to its heaviness, and they also feared about the theft and plunder of their gold.

As grains were deposited in warehouses, gold was also deposited in goldsmiths' vaults and in the vaults of other warehouse service providers for the purposes of convenience and security.

Some people, usually the goldsmiths, started the service of keeping gold safe and secure in their vaults for some charge. The owners of large quantities of gold preferred to keep their gold with the goldsmiths. The goldsmiths gave certificates or receipts to the gold depositors.

The certificates of gold were convenient to keep and carry. Some gold certificates were transferable and the owners of these certificates could claim the amount of gold mentioned on the certificates from the issuer of the certificates at any time they wanted.

The certificates issued by some well-known and reputed vault service providers and goldsmiths were easily accepted as equivalent to gold by the people. These certificates replaced gold in most of the monetary transactions where gold was used as money.

At the same time, the owners of large quantities of gold started lending their gold to people for some interest. This lending activity emerged independently of the deposit services offered by goldsmiths and vault owners.

As gold evolved as money, the two functions, namely deposits and loans of gold became prevalent. These two businesses originated independently. The gold deposit services became popular as deposit banking and the lending of gold as loan banking.

FRACTIONAL-RESERVE BANKING

In deposit banking, some goldsmiths and vault service providers whose gold certificates were acceptable as money observed that only a small fraction, say ten percent, of all the gold certificates issued by them were being redeemed by the holders of the certificates for physical gold during a period of time, for instance a year.

The deposit bankers thought that they could print more certificates than were backed by actual physical gold in their vaults and then loan those certificates to the borrowers for interest.

For example, let us consider that some people have deposited 100 ounces of gold in a deposit bank. It implies that the deposit bank must have issued gold certificates which are backed by 100 ounces of actual physical gold in the bank's vault.

Now, with the knowledge that only 10 percent of the issued certificates is being redeemed by holders of the certificates in a year, the deposit bank could lend additional certificates representing 900 ounces of gold which were not backed by 900 ounces of actual physical gold.

To understand it thoroughly, consider if only 10 percent of the issued certificates are redeemed for actual gold in a year, then it implies that a bank will need to keep only 100 ounces of physical gold in its vault for issuing certificates representing 1000 ounces of gold.

We must observe here that out of the certificates representing 1000 ounces of gold, only 10 percent of the certificates are backed by 100 ounces of actual physical gold and the remaining 90 percent which represent 900 ounces of gold are not backed by any gold.

We can see that the deposit banks and the loan banks originated independently, but the deposit banks started providing loan service too and thus evolved into banking institutions having both deposit and loan functions. The certificates issued by the banks acted as money-substitutes and were called promissory notes or banknotes.

This was a form of fractional-reserve banking in which the gold reserves were only a fraction of the total issued certificates. In modern times, the same type of fractional-reserve banking can be observed which involve fiat money in the place of gold.

CENTRAL BANKING

During the time prior to the establishment of central banks, all of the major banking institutions were owned and operated by private individuals, and the governments did not have much regulatory powers over these private banks. The governments also had to depend on these private banks for many of their financial activities.

Also, owing to the fractional-reserve nature of the banking system, sometimes situations of bank run used to arise. A bank run happens when a large number of people want to withdraw their cash from a bank and the bank does not have the required cash to give to the people.

The governments, to fulfil its expenditure needs, to have control over the private banks, and to manage bank runs, established the institutions of central banks or reserve banks. The central banks were given the exclusive rights to print and issue currency notes and to regulate the various functions of banks.

FIAT MONEY AND BANKING

Most of the central banks, in their initial phases, used to print and issue paper currency or money which were backed by physical gold and silver in their vaults. This type of paper currency was called representative money and in this system, a currency unit represented some specific quantities of either gold or silver.

Later on, as the needs and wants of the governments increased at a much higher rate than the rate at which they could mine or acquire new gold or silver, the central banks started printing more currency than were actually backed by gold or silver.

Eventually the central banks started printing paper currency without any backing of gold and silver. This type of paper currency is still continuing today and is called fiat money.

9.

INFLATION

Inflation is an increase in the total amount of money by the supply of new money in an economy at a particular time; that is to say, inflation is an increase in the total money supply at a time in an economy.

In modern economies, new money in the form of currency is printed and supplied by the central banks. Commercial banks also create new money in the form of bank loans. Bank loans are a type of money called credit money, which are essentially money-substitutes and are same as money-substitutes or balances in deposit accounts. These are the two methods by which new money is supplied in an economy.

It is self evident that the central banks and the commercial banks first create new money and become the owners of the newly created money and then loan the new money to borrowers.

CONSEQUENCES OF INFLATION

The supply of new money in an economy brings about changes in the relative purchasing power of the owners of the existing money and the receivers of the new money.

The relative purchasing power of a person is the ratio of the money owned by the person to the total money in the economy at a time, m/M.

If new money is supplied in the economy, the total money M in the economy will increase but the money owned by the people will increase only for those who receive a part of the new money, and for the remaining people the money owned will remain the same as before.

It is quite evident that the relative purchasing powers of the persons who do not receive any part of the new money will decrease. For those persons who receive new money, their new relative purchasing power will depend on the new ratio, that is the ratio of the total money they own after receiving a part of the new money to the total money which includes the newly supplied money in the economy.

Let us consider that the total money in the economy is increased by p percent, then the following four cases will arise:

1. For those who do not get any part of the new money, their relative purchasing powers will decrease.

2. For those who get a part of the new money, if the percentage increase in their money is less than p percent, then also their relative purchasing powers will decrease.

3. For those who get a part of the new money, if the percentage increase in their money is equal to p percent, then their relative purchasing powers will remain the same as before.

4. For those who get a part of the new money, if the percentage increase in their money is more than p percent, then their relative purchasing powers will increase.

10.

CONCLUSION

From reading the previous chapters of this book, it can be observed that for having a good level of material prosperity, a person must produce some valuable goods or services and for that the person must own natural resources, land, and capital goods which constitute very important factors of production.

And these factors of production must be used with the other factors of production, namely labor, time, and conducive conditions for producing the goods or services for the purpose of self consumption, or gift, or obtaining other goods and services in exchange.

From the concept of money and its relative purchasing power, it is quite manifest that inflation or the addition of new money in an economy will have no effect on the relative purchasing powers of people if the new money is distributed to the people in such a manner that the total money in the economy and every person's money in the economy are increased by the same percentage at the same time.

To understand this, consider that there are three persons A, B, and C in an economy having 100 units, 200 units, and 300 units money respectively. The total money in the economy is 600 units.

If everyone's money and the total money in the economy is increased by 10 percent at the same time, then the money owned by A, B, and C will become 110 units, 220 units, and 330 units respectively. And the total money in the economy will become 660 units.

Before inflation:

The relative purchasing power of A was
100/600 = 1/6.

The relative purchasing power of B was
200/600 = 2/6.

The relative purchasing power of C was
300/600 = 3/6.

After inflation:

The relative purchasing power of A is
110/660 = 1/6.

The relative purchasing power of B is
220/660 = 2/6.

The relative purchasing power of C is
330/660 = 3/6.

We can observe from the above information that the relative purchasing powers, that is the ratio m/M of A (1/6) , B (2/6), and C (3/6), remains the same before and after the inflation.

Now, consider a case of inflation in which the total money in the economy increases by p percent, and the new money is distributed to different groups of people in the following way:

1. In the first group of persons, each person's money increases by more than p percent.

2. In the second group of persons, each

person's money increases by p percent.

3. In the third group of persons, each person's money increases by by less than p percent.

4. And in the fourth group of the remaining persons, each person's money does not increase at all.

After inflation, the relative purchasing powers of the different groups of people will change in the following way:

1. In the first group, the relative purchasing power of each person will increase after inflation.

2. In the second group, the relative purchasing power of each person will remain the same as it was before inflation.

3. In the third group, the relative purchasing power of each person will decrease after inflation.

4. In the fourth group, the relative purchasing power of each person will also decrease after inflation.

Since the sum of the relative purchasing powers of each person's money in an economy at a time is always equal to one, it implies that the amount of decrease in the relative purchasing powers of some persons will always be equal to the amount of increase in the relative purchasing powers of other persons in the economy.

Printed in Great Britain
by Amazon